TO SAIL
NO MORE

PART FIVE

ROSS GILLETT & VIC JEFFERY

Introduction

This edition of To Sail No More Part 5 - covering the Royal Australian Navy is a natural progression from the earlier volumes. The Australian Fleet was formally created on 10 July 1911 and in the 90 years since has maintained its numerous links with the Royal Navy through its customs, personnel and ships.

The fleet that arrived in Sydney Harbour on 4 October 1913, included the Indefatigible class battlecruiser AUSTRALIA, the Bristol class light cruisers SYDNEY and MELBOURNE, the former HMS ENCOUNTER and three I-class (modified River) torpedo boat destroyers. Over the ensuing decades many former Royal Navy or British designed warships were acquired.

For the RAN its largest and most impressive warship, AUSTRALIA, became the first "To sail no more" when she was ceremonially scuttled off the Sydney coastline before a "fleet" of passenger ferries and other Men-o-war on 12 April 1924. This scuttling began a convenient method of disposal, as in the Royal Navy, when a proud warship ended her days in such an inglorious manner.

Ships laid up in reserve anchorages around Australia became a common sight in the post Second World War period, but to ensure a complete picture of the RAN's reserve fleets and ultimate disposal techniques, this book begins in 1924 and highlights the major ships up to, and including, the departure for scuttling of the guided missile destroyer PERTH in December 1999.

The authors have depicted the last departures of many ships, warships laid up in reserve and their final fates, including scrapping, scuttling or those used for target practice.

Reserve fleets were established in a number of key ports during the different decades. The most important were at Sydney, with six locations within the famous harbour, Melbourne and Brisbane, with Careening Bay at Garden Island in Western Australia (the site of the present day Fleet Base West), a major reserve facility from the late 1940s to mid 1950s and again from the early 1980s.

Some of the more graphic images in this edition of To Sail No More, taken in the last decade of the 20th century, depict the end of the River or Type 12 class frigates off Western Australia and the demise of the Oberon class submarines. The RAN's largest ship disposals in the post 1945 era included the County class heavy cruisers AUSTRALIA and SHROPSHIRE, light cruiser HOBART, aircraft carriers SYDNEY and MELBOURNE and the support vessels SUPPLY and STALWART. With few exceptions the ships depicted within these covers were British built or designed, most of which served long careers for Australia.

Acknowledgments: Royal Australian Navy photographers, past and present, Messrs Ron Hart, Brian Morrison, John Mortimer and Joe Straczek, Navy archives and the authors' private collections.

Vic Jeffery, Ross Gillett

Still looking majestic laid up in reserve in Farm Cove, Sydney during 1923, the Indefatigable class battlecruiser AUSTRALIA. The ship was active from 1911 until decommissioned on 12 December 1921.

Alongside Garden Island in 1923, workmen dismantle a considerable quantity of lead, copper, pipes and fittings aboard AUSTRALIA. The "bits and pieces" lie in tangled heaps on her decks. Below, havoc was wrought by withdrawing all piping and loose fittings, pending the final decision as to her disposal by scuttling.

The Battlecruiser AUSTRALIA - the final moment. The grand flagship was scuttled off Sydney on Saturday, 12 April 1924 under the terms the Washington Naval Treaty. The cruiser in the foreground is MELBOURNE with the Australian Prime Minister Mr Bruce embarked.

Garden Island 1922, with the two former Royal Navy / RAN cruisers PIONEER and PSYCHE lying alongside the island's eastern shoreline during their service as accommodation ships. After service in the Great War PIONEER was scuttled off Sydney on 18 February 1930 and PSYCHE's hull eventually hulked in Salamander Bay, Port Stephens, New South Wales (after brief duties as a timber barge) in 1922.

In 1926, the former Victorian colonial iron coast defence turret ship (monitor), later the RAN depot ship CERBERUS, was sunk as a breakwater at Black Rock in Port Philip Bay, Melbourne. Her rusting remains are still visible today (2000).

Another reminder of the RAN's earliest days. The remains of the submarine HMS / HMAS J3 at Swan Island, near the entrance to Port Philip in Victoria. After a very short and rather uneventful Australian naval career, the boat was sold on 24 April 1924 and scuttled off Swan Island in 1926. J3 and her sister J4 were the only Welsh built vessels (Pembroke Dockyard, South Wales) to have served in the RAN.

The River class torpedo boat destroyer (TBD) TORRENS was sunk as target practice by the heavy cruiser HMAS CANBERRA on 24 November 1930. One of six TBDs built for the RAN between 1910 and 1916, the class was modelled on the Royal Navy's I class.

After a Royal Navy career from 1905 to 1912 and service in the RAN to 1923, ENCOUNTER was employed as the static depot ship PENGUIN at Garden Island in Sydney. She is depicted here alongside the south-east corner of the island, painted white and with her armament removed. The large building behind the ship now houses the RAN Chapel.

PENGUIN (ex ENCOUNTER) is scuttled off Sydney on 14 September 1932.

11

The S class destroyer TATTOO laid up in Rushcutters Bay, Sydney Harbour in the early 1930s. Five of the former Royal Navy ships were transferred to the RAN in 1919 as part of the "Gift Fleet" (destroyer leader ANZAC, five S class, six J class submarines and three Flower class minesweepers).

The Flower class minesweeper GERANIUM makes a dramatic sight as she is scuttled off Sydney on 24 April 1935. Her two sisters, MALLOW and MARGUERITE were also scuttled on 1 August. GERANIUM saw service with the Royal Navy in the Great War and then with the RAN as a minesweeper and later as a survey ship.

The former Royal Navy Marksman class destroyer leader ANZAC is sunk as a target off the Sydney beaches on 7 May 1936. ANZAC was the only three funnelled destroyer to serve with the RAN.

Garden Island, 1 March 1937. With the seaplane carrier ALBATROSS in the background, three S class destroyers are stripped of gear prior to them being scuttled off Sydney.

After being stripped, four of the S class were laid up in Berry's Bay, Sydney in 1937, near the site of the present day mine warfare establishment HMAS Waterhen.

By 1937 the training ship TINGIRA was 71 years old. A former clipper ship named SOBRAON, TINGIRA was anchored in Rose Bay, Sydney as a cadet training ship between 1911 and 1927. After her sale she was moved up harbour, her condition gradually deteriorating over the next decade.

A rather blurry, but historic shot of Royal Navy XE craft midget submarines laid up in Woolloomooloo Bay. Photographed in 1946, the boats were disposed of locally by scrapping.

18

One of the RAN's 35 Fairmile B Motor Launches being dismantled on the slipway at the naval hospital in Sydney's Middle Harbour. Two of the class were lost in the Second World War and the remainder sold in the late 1940s.

A veteran of two world wars, the examination vessel (WW I), later Army training ship (WW 2), CAPTAIN COOK being scuttled off Sydney on 3 October 1947. She was last employed as a static training ship for Sea Scouts.

A trio of Fairmiles sit peacefully at their buoys in the Canning River, Perth in Western Australia in May 1948. ML 812 and her two sister ships are seen stripped of their weapons, radars and other fittings prior to their disposal. Ironically, the vast majority of the 33 surviving Fairmile "fleet" continued in service for many decades as tourist vessels, whale catchers and even State Government official craft.

During the Second World War, the Flotilla Leader HMAS (ex HMS) STUART served with the Mediterranean Fleet and later in the Pacific Ocean as a fast transport for Australian and Allied troops. By 1948, when this photograph was taken, STUART was 30 years old. Years later she was broken up and her hull deposited on mud flats in the upper reaches of Sydney Harbour.

A pair of Bathurst class Australian Minesweepers (AMS), better known as corvettes, lay alongside a Pyrmont Wharf in Sydney Harbour during the late 1940s. BENITA, ex HMAS GOULBURN and CARMENCITA, ex HMS BALLARAT had been sold to Hong Kong commercial interests under the Honduran flag. Following the outbreak of the Korean War, the Government would not release the ships for delivery in case after re-sale both fell into the hands of Communist forces. Both were broken up at Iron Cove in Sydney from November 1953.

Watsons Bay, just inside the entrance to Sydney Harbour, provided a safe anchorage from storms and heavy seas. In this 1948 view three Bathurst class corvettes share the long single pier with an American built tug, two motor lighters, some general purpose vessels and four Fairmiles.

The Freemantle Detachment of the Reserve Fleet laid-up in Careening Bay, Garden Island, Western Australia in 1948. Nine Bathurst class vessels were laid up here.

Not from the RAN, but the old Dutch East Indies submarine KXII on the rocks at Fairlight, located on the northern side of Sydney Harbour, in 1949. After being used as a tourist attraction, the 1922 vintage boat was blown ashore before being scrapped on the shores of the Parramatta River at Ryde.

A busy Garden Island in late 1952. In the foreground alongside the Cruiser Wharf lies a decommissioned LST 3 class tank landing ship and the ex-RN destroyer QUALITY. An oil fuel lighter lies alongside the LST. The six LST 3 vessels served only brief careers in the RAN, proving more of a nuisance, breaking down on numerous occasions, than a tactical amphibious capability. The upper decks of QUALITY are seen stripped down and guns removed. Parts from the destroyer were later used for spares for the four Q class (Type 15) frigate conversions.

Athol Bight, Sydney Harbour in 1952. From left to right, the heavy cruiser SHROPSHIRE, destroyer QUALITY, two Bathurst class corvettes and three of the LST 3 class. SHROPSHIRE transferred to the RAN in 1943 following the loss of the 1928 vintage CANBERRA at Savo Island on 9 August 1942. SHROPSHIRE was towed from Sydney Harbour in November 1954 to be broken up at Inverkiething in Scotland, after which her hull was towed to the Tyne to be dismantled.

Another view of Athol Bight on 30 May 1952. Four Bathurst class corvettes lie at the "dolphins" with the three LSTs (LABUAN nearest). DUBBO (M 251) is on the right.

After being partially stripped, LST 3022 heads out of Sydney in September 1954, bound for Brisbane to be converted to the shell dredge CORAL.

The Q class destroyer QUEENBOROUGH laid up in Watsons Bay in Sydney Harbour with the long serving depot ship PLATYPUS (right). PLATYPUS served with the RAN between 1917 and 1956, after operations with the Royal Navy in the Great War. Her time with the British included service as a submarine depot ship before being commissioned into the RAN on 13 March 1919. In April PLATYPUS sailed from Portsmouth for Australia, as escort for the six J class submarines donated to the RAN.

A view taken of the port side of the River class frigate HAWKESBURY, laid up in Watsons Bay, alongside PLATYPUS. The frigate's guns and equipment are cocooned. HAWKESBURY was sold in September 1961 and towed out of Port Jackson on 12 September 1962 to be broken up in Japan.

The County class heavy cruiser AUSTRALIA, her name painted on her starboard bow, lies patiently at her moorings in Sydney Harbour before departing under tow for the United Kingdom and scrapping. AUSTRALIA had originally commissioned in the UK on 24 April 1928. After a very active career in World War Two she served as a training ship between 1947 and 1954. She departed Sydney for the final time, under tow on 26 March 1955.

The corvette GLENELG's four-inch gun is removed in 1956 as the ship is stripped at the Palm Beach naval jetty, Rockingham, Western Australia. The ship was sold for scrap in May 1957 to Hong Kong Rolling Mills, together with her sisters KATOOMBA and PARKES.

The old and the new, 1956 style. AUSTRALIA arrives in Barrow-in-Furness (UK) for scrapping and is pulled past the new light fleet aircraft carrier MELBOURNE, still fitting out.

The former RAN Bathurst class corvettes LITHGOW (M206) and DELORAINE with the Dutch ocean-going tug LOIRE alongside, are prepared for their final voyage to Hong Kong shipbreakers. They are seen here on 8 August 1956, at the Port of Fremantle outer harbour.

Bathurst class corvettes lie alongside the Oil Wharf at Garden Island, Sydney Harbour, New South Wales.

Six Bathurst class corvettes in retirement. The group were laid up in Iron Cove, west of the city of Sydney in the 1950s. All were later sold.

The Modified Leander class light cruiser HOBART berthed at the Oil Wharf, Garden Island. Outboard of her is the Q class destroyer QUALITY.

PLATYPUS is towed down Sydney Harbour. The 40 year old vessel had served the RAN in numerous roles including depot and repair, base and training ship until finally decommissioned on 1 November 1956. She was towed from Sydney in 1958 and broken up in Japan.

The end of an era. The last three ships of the former Fremantle Detachment of the RAN Reserve Fleet in Gage Roads off Fremantle, Western Australia, are prepared for their final voyage to the Japanese shipbreakers. The former PARKES (M361), and GLENELG have the ocean-going tug BUSTLER alongside whilst the Fremantle tug WYOLA moves KATOOMBA into position. Photographed on 27 November 1957.

A waterline shot of Athol Bight, with the sloop SWAN (left) and two corvettes. (ARARAT centre) in the late 1950s.

Three Bathurst class corvettes and the light fleet carrier SYDNEY at the Athol Bight "dolphins" in the late 1950s. The moorings were finally removed in the mid 1990s.

The Bar class boom defence vessels (KARANGI on left) at the Boom Depot, Waverton, Sydney in 1960. The trio were originally commissioned in 1940-41 and operated mainly from Darwin in the Northern Territory during the Second World War. One of the vessels, KANGAROO was later hulked in Homebush Bay, her hull still protruding above the surface today (2000).

On 11 October 1960, the armament stores ship WOOMERA exploded while dumping obsolete ammunition off Sydney. Four crew members were lost in the accident. WOOMERA was completed as AV 1356 in November 1945, a wooden stores ship for the Australian Army. She was transferred to the RAN in February 1946.

An excellent aerial view of Sydney Harbour on Australia Day, 26 January 1961. Laid up in Athol Bight are the aircraft carrier SYDNEY and the cruiser HOBART, two destroyers and two frigates opposite SYDNEY, six corvettes (centre) and two frigates each side of HOBART.

Watsons Bay, 12 June 1962. Six RAN vessels of various sizes lie alongside the wooden wharf. From left; a 40 foot workboat, two general purpose vessels, a Bathurst class corvette, PLATYPUS and the River class frigate GASCOYNE. The black hull on the far left is the former Second World War examination vessel CAPTAIN COOK (III).

The Battle cass destroyer TOBRUK lies alongside Athol Bight in Sydney Harbour with the Tribal class destroyers ARUNTA and WARRAMUNGA. TOBRUK served in the RAN from 1950 to 1960, retired early after the arrival of the improved Daring class destroyers VOYAGER, VAMPIRE and VENDETTA. She was eventually towed from Sydney on 10 April 1972 and broken up in Japan.

The remains of the Bathurst class corvette GYMPIE in the process of being scrapped in Rozelle Bay, Sydney in 1962.

The River class frigate HAWKESBURY and Modified River class frigate MURCHISON lie totally neglected at Sydney's Athol Bight "dolphins" in September 1962. The decision to sell the two ships had been made and they departed Sydney a few days later on 12 September.

"End of an Era" for two Commonwealth light cruisers, the modified Leander class HMAS HOBART (ex-HMS APOLLO) and the modified Dido class HMNZS BLACK PRINCE (ex-RN) pictured in the Miyachi shipbreaking yard at Osaka, Japan in 1962. Scrapping is well advanced on HOBART but has yet to commence on BLACK PRINCE.

A fine starboard quarter view of the Tribal class destroyer WARRAMUNGA. The ship is shown as converted to an anti-submarine destroyer at Garden Island in Sydney. After decommissioning on 7 November 1959 WARRAMUNGA was removed from her reserve fleet berth and towed from Sydney to Japan in May 1963

Inactive ships still need their bottoms scraped and sides painted. ARUNTA (left) and TOBRUK (right) share the Captain Cook Dry Dock at Garden Island in 1963. Note the bare decks of both destroyers after their years laid up in reserve.

The former corvette HMAS CASTLEMAINE alongside the shore establishment HMAS CERBERUS at Westernport, Victoria. Commissioned on 17 June 1942, she served as an escort between Australia and New Guinea before paying-off into reserve in 1945. In 1958 she was disarmed, refitted and returned to service as a static training ship, a role she fulfilled until 1971. In September 1973 it was announced that she was to be presented to the Maritime Trust of Australia for preservation as a museum ship. Today (2000), fully restored, CASTLEMAINE is berthed at Williamstown in Victoria.

The RANR stationary training ship MILDURA, pictured with the General Purpose Vessel (GPV) 957 outboard, at Kangaroo Point, Brisbane, Queensland. One of 56 Bathurst-class corvettes built for the RAN between 1940-44, she was commissioned on 22 July, 1941 and served with Pacific east coast convoys during the war. Postwar she was employed at Hong Kong on escort duties before clearing mines from Australian, New Guinea and Solomon Islands waters. Paid-off in 1948 at Fremantle, the corvette was brought forward as a National Service training ship, serving between 1951-53, before her transfer to Brisbane. MILDURA was sold on 8 September 1965 and broken-up locally.

The former HMAS BARWON, with six corvettes of the Bathurst class, laid up in Athol Bight, Sydney. An unidentified River class frigate lies behind BARWON.

WARREGO, the last of four Grimsby class sloops of the RAN, being broken up in the Sydney Harbour backwater of Rozelle Bay in 1966. After her years in commission during the Second World War, the sloop operated as a survey ship from 1945 until her decommissioning on 15 August 1963.

The former boom defence vessel KOOKABURRA rests on the bottom after sinking at her moorings in Rozelle Bay, Sydney in February, 1967 whilst awaiting scrapping. Raised in 1970, she was towed out to sea and scuttled.

The famous wartime Tribal class destroyer ARUNTA laid up at Sydney in 1968. Despite being modernised as an anti-submarine destroyer between 1950 and 1952, she was paid off on 14 June 1956. The destroyer was inactive for over 11 years before being towed to her watery grave. She was the last survivor of the three Tribal class built for the RAN during WW 2.

ARUNTA passes under the Sydney Harbour Bridge enroute to the Chinese shipbreakers at Taipei on 12 February 1969. Shortly after clearing Port Jackson, ARUNTA unexplainably began to take in water and developed a list, sinking the following day, about 60 nautical miles north-east of Broken Bay, New South Wales.

Two former RAN warships, the Q class frigate QUIBERON (centre) and the Battle class destroyer TOBRUK are towed out of Sydney by the Japanese tug SUMI MARU No.18 on 10 April 1972. Purchased by the Fujita Salvage Co. they were towed to Moji, Japan and broken-up.

The remains of the first vessel launched for the Commonwealth Naval Forces, later designated the Royal Australian Navy - the torpedo boat destroyer PARRAMATTA in the early 1970s. Seen lying on a mudbank north of Milson Island in the Hawkesbury River, New South Wales. A public appeal saw her bow section removed and erected at Garden Island in Sydney. HRH, The Duke of Edinburgh unveiled the PARRAMATTA Memorial on 31 October 1988.

The former RAN training ship QUEENBOROUGH laid-up in Athol Bight, Sydney, in 1973 with the oil fuel lighter OFL 1202 outboard. Laid down as the Royal Navy Q class destroyer HMS QUEENBOROUGH and commissioned in 1942, she was transferred to the RAN on 29 October 1945. Converted to an anti-submarine frigate in 1950, she ended her days as a training ship, before being sold out of service for breaking up - on 8 August 1975.

The veteran RAN Battle class destroyer and later training ship ANZAC is towed out of Sydney Harbour in 1975. Commissioned in 1950, the Korean War veteran was decommissioned on 4 October 1974.

The battered remains of the Attack class patrol boat HMAS ARROW in 1975 after she was driven under a wharf and foundered during Cyclone Tracy at Darwin on Christmas Day 1974. Two crew members were lost. ARROW was officially written-off on 7 February 1975 and subsequently broken up.

The former HMAS DOOMBA (ex HMS WEXFORD), an RAN auxiliary minesweeper and former Royal Navy Great War Hunt class minesweeper, is scuttled off the New South Wales coast in December 1976. Sold out of the Royal Navy in 1921 the vessel was rebuilt as a river steamer and renamed DOOMBA. She began her new commercial career in 1923 operating mainly along the Brisbane River and into Moreton Bay. DOOMBA was requisitioned by the RAN on 3 September 1939 and commissioned as HMAS DOOMBA 22 days later. Paid-off on 13 March 1945 she was stripped and converted into a dumb lighter. She was laid-up in 1970 prior to being scuttled.

The former aircraft carrier and later fast troop transport SYDNEY (III) being towed out of Sydney Harbour by the Japanese tug TOKUEI MARU No. 27 on 23 December 1975 bound for South Korean shipbreakers.

The long tow to South Korea gets underway.

The decommissioned and stripped Daring class destroyer VENDETTA is towed from Garden Island to the Athol Bight "dolphins" in Sydney Harbour by the naval tug HTS 501 on 9 October 1979.

The Daring class destroyers VENDETTA (08) and DUCHESS (154), with the oceanographic research ship and former River class frigate DIAMANTINA at the Athol Bight "dolphins" at Sydney in 1980.

The former HMAS DUCHESS after her conversion from a Daring class destroyer to a training ship, being moved up Harbour by the ocean-going tug SUMI MARU on 4 June 1980. She was later towed to the shipbreakers in Taiwan on 9 July. DUCHESS was loaned to the RAN - by the Royal Navy - after the loss of HMAS VOYAGER in 1964 and purchased outright in 1972. On the left is the stern of the destroyer escort HMAS DERWENT and on the right, the bow of the destroyer escort HMAS TORRENS.

The Daring class destroyer VENDETTA stripped and laid-up at the Athol Bight "dolphins" in Sydney Harbour on 5 November 1983. She is flanked by the former flagship and aircraft carrier MELBOURNE.

The new guided missile frigate HMAS SYDNEY (IV) passes MELBOURNE and the decommissioned Daring class destroyer VENDETTA, as she arrives on her delivery voyage from the USA in March 1984.

MELBOURNE is moved away from her moorings at the Athol Bight "dolphins" on 27 April 1985 in preparation for her long tow to Shanghai, China. She was broken-up at Dalian after being purchased by the China United Shipping Company.

COLAC, the former Second World War corvette, later converted to a tank-cleaning vessel is towed down the New South Wales coast for her final role as a submarine target. HMAS OVENS sank COLAC on 4 March 1987.

The River class frigate DIAMANTINA flies the Red Ensign as she departs for the Queensland Maritime Museum on 1 October 1980. Gifted by the Federal Government, today (2000) she survives as a museum ship in Brisbane after restoration to her 1945 appearance.

A 1988 view of the former RAN Ton class minesweeper IBIS (ex-HMS SINGLETON) alongside at Pyrmont in Sydney after her sale in 1985. Her sistership, SNIPE (ex-HMS ALCASTON) is astern of her.

The 4.5 inch gun turret from the decommissioned River class destroyer escort PARRAMATTA is removed at the Garden Island dockyard, Sydney in 1991 for re-location to the RAN Historical Repository at Spectacle Island. The ship's Ikara and Seacat missile launchers were also moved to the site.

The 1941 Bathurst class corvette WHYALLA is moved ashore to her final resting place in Whyalla, South Australia (where she was originally built). Sold out of naval service in 1947 to the Melbourne Harbour Board, she was renamed RIP and had her configuration altered. WHYALLA was gifted to the City to be converted back to her original wartime appearance.

Leaving an Australian port for the last time, the former River class destroyer escort PARRAMATTA is towed out of the Port of Fremantle enroute to Pakistani shipbreakers on 13 March 1992. PARRAMATTA had departed Sydney five months earlier but mechanical problems plagued the tug WOOREE during its southern transit of the Australian coast. Both vessels were later broken-up in Pakistan.

After eight months swinging around a buoy in Cockburn Sound, Western Australia, the former River class destroyer escort STUART is towed away by the tug CTW EAGLE on 7 May 1992 bound for Singapore shipbreakers. STUART's twin 4.5-inch gun turret today stands outside the Fleet Base, HMAS Stirling in Western Australia. Her foremast was erected at the Naval Reserve Cadet unit TS Canning and her mainmast gifted to the nearby Cockburn Sea Rescue Group.

The hull of the former RAN Oberon class submarine OXLEY, is towed from HMAS Stirling across Cockburn Sound in Western Australia to be broken up at Henderson by Australian Shipbuilding Industries. The tow was performed by the Navy tugs TAMMAR (forward) and QUOKKA (aft) on 9 March 1992. Lying peacefully in the background is the decommissioned destroyer escort STUART.

OXLEY in an advanced state of demolition in the yards of Australian Shipbuilding Industries at Henderson during September 1992. OXLEY's fin still survives, erected outside the RAN Submarine Systems and Training Centre at the nearby HMAS Stirling - Fleet Base West.

There she blows! The former RAN River class destroyer escort DERWENT is scuttled by demolition charges set by Australian Clearance Diving Team 4, west of Rottnest Island off the West Australian coast on 21 December 1994.

The battered DERWENT had been subjected to a series of ship survivability tests and since her sinking has proved to be a successful "fish attraction device".

The former Oberon class submarine OTWAY being broken up in Sydney
Harbour on 19 December 1995.

OTWAY's entire casing was removed and relocated to Holbrook in southern New South Wales as a memorial and tourist attraction.

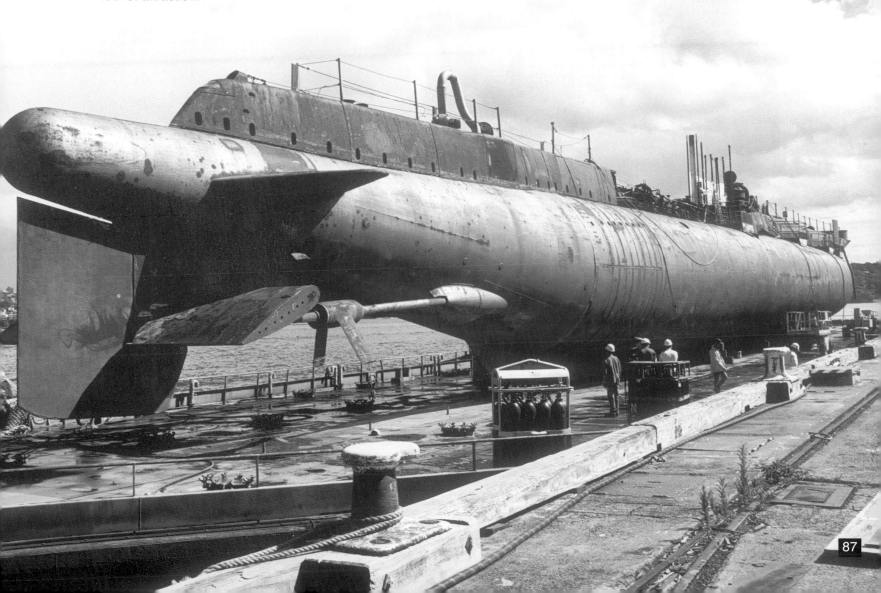

The stripped hulk of the former River class destroyer escort SWAN laid-up in a backwater of the Port of Bunbury, Western Australia. The ship was awaiting her final voyage south to Dunsborough to be sunk as a dive wreck on 14 December 1997.

Should you ever doubt the power of a modern torpedo, the following sequence of pictures will prove very sobering. Australias last Type 12 Destroyer Escort, TORRENS, ended her days as a submarine target off the West Australian coast. She was sunk by a Mk 48 wire-guided torpedo fired from over the horizon by the submarine FARNCOMB on 14 June 1999.

The blast has blown the superstructure clear of the ship. The plume of water and debris is reported to have reached 150 metres. Was this really the work of one torpedo or were there explosives onboard to make a "bigger bang"?

With the blast still subsiding it is already obvious that the ship has broken in two. The bows and the stern roll in opposite directions.

The Oberon class submarine HMAS OVENS flying her paying-off pendant, approaches HMAS Stirling (Fleet Base West). Decommissioned on 21 March 1987, OVENS was used as an alongside training submarine until 1998. Gifted to the West Australian Government, she was towed to Fremantle on 17 November 1998 and today (2000) is slipped on the WW 2 vintage South Mole slipway as part of the West Australian Maritime Museum.

ONSLOW, 15 April 1999, is towed towards her new home, the Australian National Maritime Museum in Sydney. The boat is now preserved alongside the Daring class destroyer VAMPIRE. Having secured special permission, both vessels still fly the Australian White Ensign.

The former HMAS MORESBY, a hydrographic survey ship, is towed away from HMAS Stirling in Western Australia on 27 October 1999 after being sold to Hong Kong interests. Decommissioned on 13 November 1997, MORESBY had been the first RAN ship to achieve the milestone of sailing a million nautical miles in her 33-year career. She has since been converted to the role of a refugee ship and renamed PATRICIA ANNE HOTUNG and has operated in the Far East around East Timor.

The decommissioned PERTH was towed from Sydney on 14 December 1999 bound for Albany on the southern West Australian coast. The ship was expected to be sunk as a dive wreck in 2001.

INDEX